Marvelous
Manifestation Mandalas

Color It True

Adult Coloring Books that Draw Good Things to You!

1

RUTH SHILLING

All One World Books & Media

Other books by Ruth Shilling:

- **MAGNETIC Manifestation Mandalas**: "Color It True" Adult Coloring Books that Draw Good Things to You, Volume 2. Published 2016. ISBN : 978-0-9971991-2-3

- **MIRACULOUS Manifestation Mandalas**: "Color It True" Adult Coloring Books that Draw Good Things to You, Volume 3. Published 2016. ISBN : 978-0-9971991-3-0

- **MAGNIFICENT Manifestation Mandalas**: "Color It True" Adult Coloring Books that Draw Good Things to You, Volume 4. Published 2016. ISBN : 978-0-9971991-4-7

- **Success with the Violin and Life**: Strategies, Techniques and Tips for Learning Quickly and Doing Well. Published by All One World Books & Media, 2016. ISBN : 978-0-9971991-0-9

- **VIBRATO**: Playing the Violin & Viola with Vibrato (ebook).

- **TONE**: Violin & Viola Bowing Techniques for a Rich, Satisfying Sound (ebook).

- **SINAI**: The Desert & Bedouins of South Sinai's Central Regions. Published by Palm Press, Cairo, Egypt, 2003. ISBN 978-9-7750895-2-6

Cover, text and mandala designs: Ruth Shilling

Published by All One World Books & Media
Wakefield, RI, USA
all1world.com

ISBN : 978-0-9971991-1-6

PRINTED IN THE UNITED STATES OF AMERICA

Using the Marvelous Manifestation Mandalas

The Marvelous Manifestation Mandalas are specially designed to bring about good things for you!

Here are some of the ways to use them:

- Bringing more of what you enjoy and desire into your life
- Getting clarity on questions, decisions or how to handle situations
- Sending healing, power or prayers to people and animals you care about
- As a gratitude meditation or to give your affirmations a boost
- For cards of appreciation, birthdays or other celebrations

In the Center of the Mandala

The center of each mandala is an open space for you to put a statement, symbol or picture that will be the focus. That intention will flow through as you are enjoying the coloring. Here are suggestions of what to put in the center:

- A short statement (see tips below)
- A symbol that has meaning to you
- A picture or photo

The Process

The more you enjoy yourself as you do the coloring, the better it is. The more **light, fun, playful, relaxed, easy going and upbeat** you feel, the more easily whatever you are focusing on can come about. If there is music that makes you feel good or something else you like, listening as you color will make it even more fun!

The key to the manifestation process is to be in that easy, fluid state that most of us find ourselves in as we choose the colors and fill in the spaces between the lines. And if you like to color outside the lines, that's OK, too! This is your time to do it just the way you feel it. No one else's rules, just whatever you feel in the moment.

Desired Outcome

Put your Desired Outcome statement or picture in the center, then color in the Mandala. As you color, your effortless enjoyment of the activity will set in motion the fulfillment of your desired outcome. No need for tension or *TRYING* (that just messes it up). It is said that "to enter the kingdom of heaven, become like a child."

The kingdom is where all this wonderful stuff is just waiting for us. Just having fun as you color the mandalas is a delightful pathway to access it.

Clarity

Not sure what you want to manifest? Write, "What would be a good focus for me?" at the top of the page (not in the center of the mandala), then start coloring with the intent that you will get clear at some point as you go along. Add the answer in the center whenever it comes to you, and then finish the mandala. If nothing comes as you color, then just write (in the center) the next thing that comes into your mind when you finish. Let it just pop into your mind spontaneously. It will be a clue to your answer.

You can also ask about how to handle a situation, an upcoming decision or some other question. If you are unsure about how to word it, a good one to use is:

    "The most benevolent outcome for _____" (fill in the blank).

Sending to Someone Else*

Put the name and what you would like to send to someone else into the center, and then color the mandala.

*Note: It doesn't work out for us to have an agenda about what ought to happen for someone else. Of course, we will often want something to happen for someone, but it really isn't our choice. That can be a hard one, especially with the people we love.

However, we CAN send supportive love, healing energy, a belief in the possibilities that surround them, appreciation for who they are, an open door to our focused attention, our awareness of their magnificence, a willingness to know them as they truly are, and much more. We just don't get to decide what they choose or what their soul has chosen or what God has chosen for them... that kind of thing.

If you are ever unsure what to put in as a focus with someone, a good one to use is,

"Sending whatever is most helpful to _____" (fill in the blank).

Gratitude Meditations and Affirmations

Many people who are on the spiritual path or who are working on their personal growth have become aware of the power of gratitude to uplift our lives and pave the way to receiving more of what we enjoy and appreciate. Writing something in the center of the mandala about what you are grateful for and then doing the coloring is a delightful way to do this. And afterwards, your artwork will make a beautiful addition to your sacred space.

If you are working with affirmations, writing them in the center and then coloring the design is a good way to imbue them with some extra power.

Celebration & Appreciation Cards

The possibilities are endless for using the mandalas on cards of appreciation, birthday or celebration. Use the center to write your message and then create your unique colored-in version. It will be so much better than a store-bought card because it is especially from you and is like no other!

Note: The last three designs in the book are formatted to fold in half for making cards.

TIPS *for the Manifestation Statement in the Center*

Describe the result and how you will feel

- Choose something which is believable to you
- Include yourself
- Put it in the positive
- Do both SPECIFIC things and underlying GENERAL feelings

Statements that Describe the Result and How You will Feel

The best statements embody what it is to have the goal you have chosen. **The-state-of-having-it** is what you want to manifest. Therefore, statements are in the present, and as though it has already happened.

A statement like, "I will do well on the exam," communicates anticipation of doing well, but not actually having done well. A better statement would be, "I am so happy I did well on the exam!"

An easy way to figure out your statement is to think about what you will say to your friends or family after it happens. If you think you would say, "Guess what! I aced the exam!" then "I aced the exam!" would be a good statement in the center for you.

Choose Something which is Believable to You

If your focus is having more financial abundance, it may not be believable to you that you will be a millionaire by your next birthday. So it is better to choose something that *does* seem possible even though it has not happened yet. Maybe it is believable that you might get an increase in salary, or that you receive money in some unexpected way. A statement for that could be, "I love having this extra money!"

Once the smaller goal comes about, you can enjoy setting bigger goals as you welcome more and more abundance and possibilities into your life.

Include Yourself in the Statement

If you just write "NEW CAR," chances are that *someone* will get a new car, but it might not be you! Better would be, "I love my new car!"

Put the Statements in the Positive

This isn't about fighting the good fight, killing off the bad, and things like that. This is about choosing what you would like from the buffet of possibilities. "Yes, I would like that. Yes, that looks good to me." So the subject of the statement in the center is what you are choosing, not what you want to avoid.

"I don't have trouble with my boss anymore," actually puts the focus on having trouble. Better would be, "My boss and I get along just fine now," or "I am glad I have a good relationship with my boss." If you find yourself thinking of words like *don't, not* or *no*, write it out that way, and then switch it into a positive before you put it into the center of the mandala.

Go for Both SPECIFIC things & Underlying GENERAL Feelings

To get the optimal benefit from the Marvelous Manifestation Mandalas, color in some for specific outcomes and others for the desires that permeate your life in general.

For example, I might be wanting to have **more available money**. That is certainly a logical thing to want, and when it comes, it is a nice tangible way to see that my manifestations are having an effect.

However, if the money was just pieces of paper and could not be used to buy anything, would I want it? Probably not. So it isn't actually the money I want, but rather, the ability to get things that I want and need.

Now let's say I want to buy a nice shirt. I have other shirts already, but I have my eye on a new one that will look terrific on me. So what will that shirt bring me? A good feeling about my appearance.

So one could say the real desire is to feel good about my appearance. But what is behind that? Wanting to **feel good about myself**.

If I get the shirt, but for some reason it makes me feel bad about myself – maybe I think I paid too much, or it doesn't look so good after all – then manifesting that shirt would not be fulfilling for me.

If on the other hand, I put what I really want in the center of the mandala (feeling good about myself) and I attain that, then whether I have the shirt or not isn't all that important (though it still might be nice to have).

So choosing something specific can be very good for helping us to understand and witness that the manifestation process works (so doing it is certainly worthwhile), but what will bring us more happiness and contentment is to put into the center the desires that are underneath all the rest.

Sample Statements

Below are some statements to use as ideas, but of course it is for you to choose something in your own words that has a good feeling for YOU. It's best if the statement matches the way you think inside your own head, the thoughts you would think if something good happened.

Money and Abundance:

"Thank goodness I have that extra
$_____ a month now!"

"I love my new car!"

"It's a relief to be able to buy what
I need."

"Wow! My life is rich."

"I even have extra money now."

"I enjoy giving. I have so much now."

"I am so glad that I earned $_____,000
this year."

"There is always a lot to be grateful
for."

"I have more of everything now –
more opportunities, more people I
love, more money, more time, and
good health, too! I am so
grateful!"

"I have SO much right now."

People and Relationships*:

"I have really good friends."

"I meet lots of wonderful people."

"I like my coworkers."

"I just love being married now."

"I'm glad to have my family."

"(name) and I are doing better."

"As we get older, my marriage keeps
changing in a good way."

"I am so grateful to be with such a
wonderful partner."

*More about Relationships on the
next page.

Happiness and Contentment:

"Every day I do things I like to do."

"Every day has its own beauty."

"Thanks be."   "All is well."

"Each day there is something new to
learn, to see, to appreciate."

"I just give thanks for it all."

"I am in a good place."

"Life is so beautiful."

Self-Esteem:

"I am actually OK."

"I like having time by myself."

"I know I did it well."

"Each one of us is magnificent."

"It feels good to know I make a
difference / I can contribute."

"I like myself now."

"No one makes me laugh more
than myself!"

Sending to Others:

"Healing and Love to (name)."

"Whatever is helpful to (name)."

"Peace to you, (name)."

"Clarity and Strength to (name)."

"Love and Power is surrounding &
enfolding (name)."

"(name), you are Love."

"(name) is forever held in Love."

"(name), I love you."

"(name), I see your beauty and power."

More on Relationships

In the *Sending to Someone Else* section, it was pointed out that we don't get to choose what happens for someone else. Likewise, it doesn't work to try to manifest, "He wants xyz. He will do xyz." However, since we are half of a relationship, we CAN focus to have a relationship change.

A vivid way to see this is to imagine two people as colored-in circles. One is a yellow disk and the other is a red disk. When these disks overlap, the yellow and red make orange. So the relationship is orange. However, if the red disk changes to blue, the overlap of the yellow and blue disk will make green. The relationship is now green instead of orange.

So we have the power to change any relationship we find ourselves in. If we change, the relationship will also change. Using the mandalas can help to have those changes be ones that you feel good about.

What Goes Along with the Manifestations

To have the positive outcome that we are wanting, there is often some additional action or attitude that could help it along. For example, if my positive outcome is to have easy relations with my coworkers, it would help if my mental picture of who they are is a good one, or at least that I hold the view that it is possible for them to be easy to get along with.

If I am wanting to bring more abundance into my life, I may need to act on inspirations that come to me, welcome new contacts into my life, practice gratefully receiving what is offered to me, as well as appreciating what I already have. How do I react when someone gives me a compliment? Do I receive it or push it away? If I put "I receive extra money" into the center of the mandala, do I rejoice when I find a dime lying on the ground in front of me? If a friend picks up the tab at lunch, do I receive that gift in a graceful and appreciative way?

If I want an abundant life, part of that is to joyfully and gratefully receive.

Repeatedly receiving in a delighted way
is the fast track to abundance!

After Your Mandala is Finished

Your mandala will be beautiful and uniquely YOU! If you place your completed mandala somewhere that you will see it while you are relaxing, its power can continue to work with your subconscious mind long after you finish.

You can also put it in a sacred place or on an altar and place a candle in the center of it. Each time you light the candle it will enliven the focus of the mandala. If you use a pendulum for dowsing, you can put your pendulum over the mandala and as it spins around it will imbue your mandala with more and more energy.

Wishing you many fruitful manifestations
and
some delightful surprises, too!

Ruth Shilling

P.S.

I would love to hear your success stories and see your beautiful mandalas! If you send them to **a1w.books@gmail.com**, I well get them. Or send along a link to your YouTube video telling about it.

Facebook pages: "Flow of Well Being" and "Ruth Shilling, M.M."
Blog: flowofwellbeing.wordpress.com
More at: all1world.com

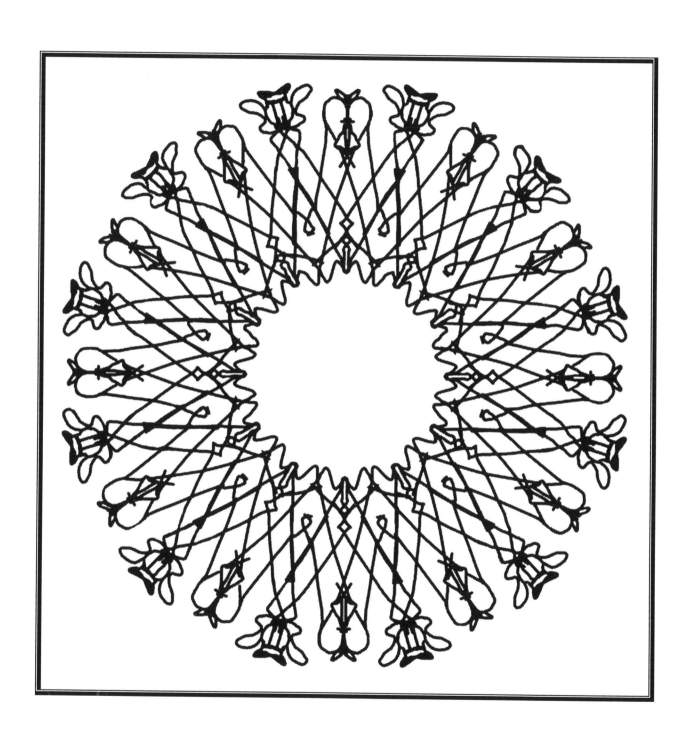

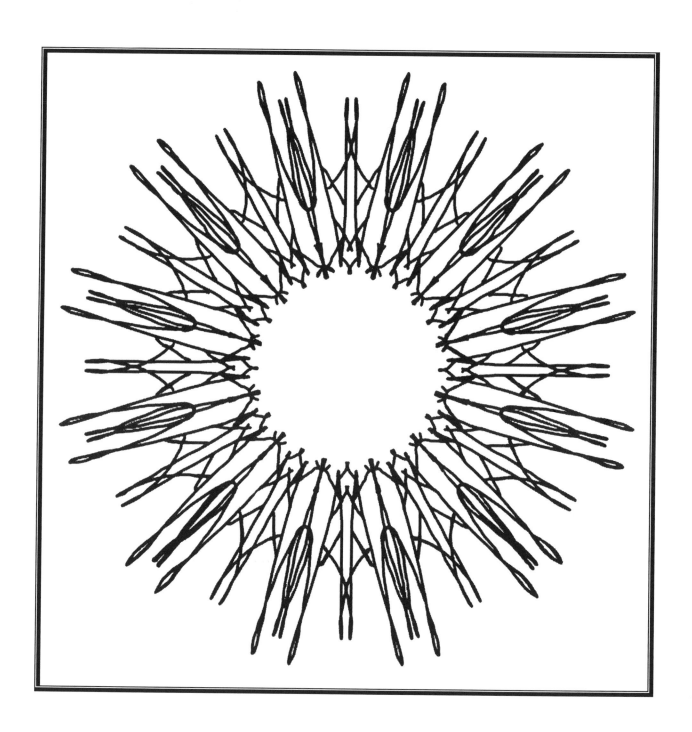

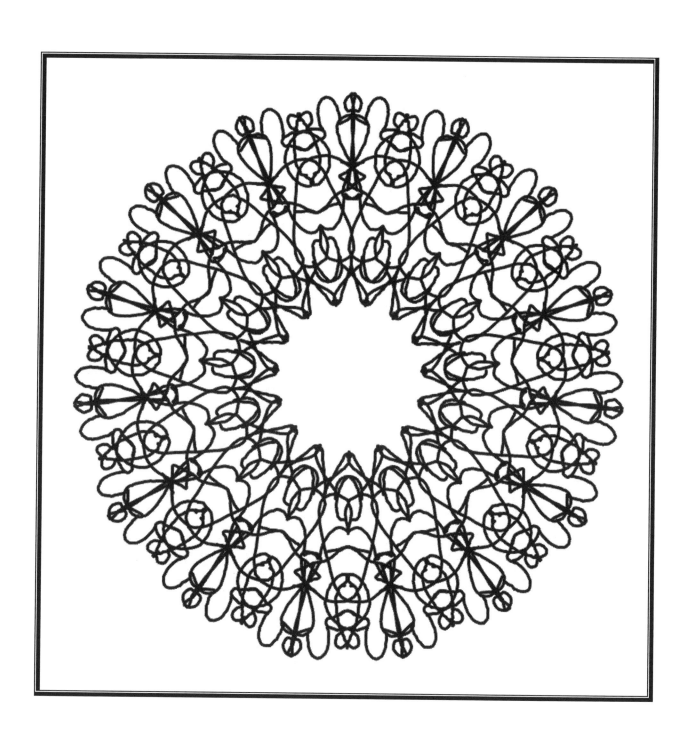

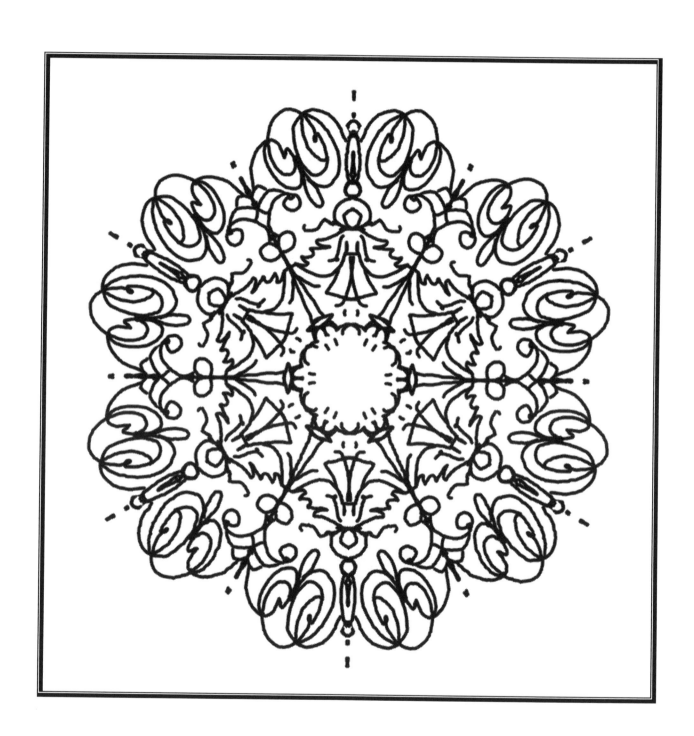

* The mandalas on the next three pages can be folded in half and made into a greeting cards. Fold along border, then trim. Permission given to scan or photocopy for your project. You can use "Invitation Envelopes" (4 3/8 x 5¾") or 4½ x 6½" envelopes. *

Photocopy or scan this page. Print on heavy paper or card stock. It is easier to trim if you fold it first.

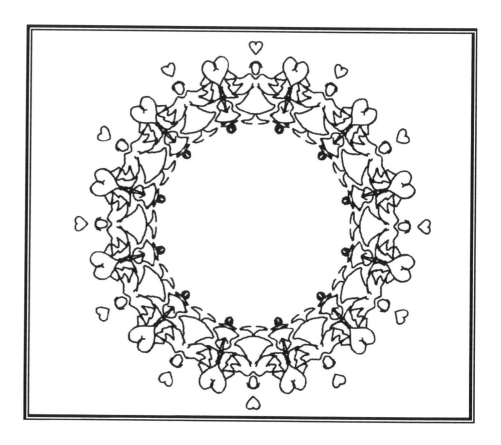

Photocopy or scan this page. Print on heavy paper or card stock. It is easier to trim if you fold it first.

Photocopy or scan this page. Print on heavy paper or card stock. It is easier to trim if you fold it first.

If you enjoyed this coloring book, there are more in this series!

MAGNETIC Manifestation Mandalas

"Color It True" Adult Coloring Books that Draw Good Things to You, Volume 2.
Published 2016. ISBN : 978-0-9971991-2-3

MIRACULOUS Manifestation Mandalas

"Color It True" Adult Coloring Books that Draw Good Things to You, Volume 3.
Published 2016. ISBN : 978-0-9971991-3-0

MAGNIFICENT Manifestation Mandalas

"Color It True" Adult Coloring Books that Draw Good Things to You, Volume 4.
Published 2016. ISBN : 978-0-9971991-4-7

Published by All One World Books & Media.
all1world.com

Made in the USA
Middletown, DE
17 April 2016